Domestic Fuel

Books by Erin Mouré:
Empire, York Street
Whisky Vigil
Wanted Alive
Domestic Fuel

ERIN MOURÉ
Domestic Fuel

ANANSI

Toronto   Buffalo   London   Sydney

The author and publisher are grateful for the support of The Canada Council and the Ontario Arts Council.

Author photo: Ken Mouré

Made in Canada for
House of Anansi Press Limited
35 Britain Street
Toronto, Ontario M5A 1R7

Canadian Cataloguing in Publication Data

Mouré, Erin, 1955–
  Domestic fuel

(House of Anansi poetry series; HAP 45)
Poems.
ISBN 0-88784-143-0.

I. Title.   II. Series.

PS8576.O892D65 1985   C811'.54   C85-098404-1
PR9199.3.M68D65 1985

Contents

A Sporting Life

Speaking In Tongues

Thaw

Domestic Fuel

Acknowledgements

Arc
Blue Buffalo
Canadian Forum
Canadian Literature
Cross-Canada Writers' Quarterly
Dandelion
Descant
Ethos
Event
Fiddlehead
Fireweed
Four By Four
Prism international
Quarry
Rubicon
Saturday Night
The Malahat Review
This Magazine
Writing
Zest

"Domestic Fuel" first appeared as a broadside published by
        Flat Singles Press, Vancouver.

Some of these poems were anthologized in:
        Anything Is Possible, ed. Mary di Michele, Mosaic Press,
        1984.
        Canadian Poetry Now: 20 Poets of the 80's, ed. Ken Norris,
        House of Anansi, 1984.
        *Women & Words: The Anthology/Les Femmes et les Mots:
        Une Anthologie,* Harbour Publishing, 1984.

A short term grant from the Canada Council in October 1983
enabled me to work on some of these poems.

Alguien limpia un fusil en su cocina.
¿ Con qué calor hablar del más allá?

Someone cleans a rifle in his kitchen.
How dare one speak about the beyond?

César Vallejo

A Sporting Life

Lunge

All of a sudden you find out there isn't enough time.
You find out there was never enough time.
You find out you shouldn't have washed the dishes.

Over & over, so many dishes, the wet cloth, the spill
across the counter, window, bird out there
or not, the clean house, begin

& you find out you shouldn't have bought the clocks.
You shouldn't have bothered buying clocks.
You never had what they had to measure.

You leap up & throw them face-down into the trash.

There is not enough time to cry about this.
The pain in your back is very deep
& pointless.
You find out that all this time they said
you were part of the working class
there was no time.
The real working class in this country was always unemployed,
& you always had a job, the same one.

You find out there is no such thing as enough time
& still you don't have any of it.
You shouldn't have craved the arms of women.
You shouldn't have slept with men.
You shouldn't have dreamed *Philosophy,* or
the heart monitor screen in your apartment bedroom,
just like in emergency.
It's all shit. Merde. This, & hey, & you others.

Time for the medicine. You fast cure. You fuck-up mad dog. You you.
You lunge over the table. In mid-lunge. Going for the adrenalin again,
going for keeps, prose, boots, the sandwich you couldn't eat, you bit &
spit out, you thought it would make you sick again. Lunge for the dog's
stale portion of sleep, your legs straight off the chair, your hair stuck out,
the clatter of the chair falling backward, zone five, zone six, the sound
of

Your arms make

Amicus, object,   referrent

Points   of or–   der

What The Woman Remembers Of Her Dying, On The Street Before The Ambulance Came

The core that eludes me, the words
un-spoken,   pulled back into the tongue.
It is the tear-space inside the wall, where
the seventy years are waiting,
their mouths round with o's.
It is the seven nights of the body.
The beginning of the spine.
Sleep without measure.
Sash flung up & down.
Outside in.
It is the air.
When it meets my face, my mouth opens.
It is not fear.
It is what we fear.
It is the green trees rushing upward from the boulevard.
It is green everywhere.
It is not the hung figure.
It is not maleness.
It is grass. It is the tree.
It is the sound of hands.

Like Theatre

A woman describes her
life as the decreasing width
of beds
King-size bed, double bed, & now single bed
Measures the air with her hands
Hot air
Islands of air
When the morning comes what does it matter
the woman ends, laughing,

& directs the music in the restaurant for her friends

Upside-down music, she says
like theatre

Shock Troop

Shock troop
shock exercise
Knife is a verb
Bayonet a verb
Coat a verb
Absolute is a conjunction
Now get up & pay for the coffee,
make a sentence, fool

She knife, she coat, absolute she bayonet
he said
incomprehensible as
shock troops blowing the door in
& taking the TV down stairs to a truck

You don't pay me, you live here
she said, pushing his money back, the tip, too

Poem Rejected By The Globe & Mail

One dream or another.
The belly fat bent over, a body poised on the lakeshore.
Sleep, industry!
Sleep, Ontario.
Your punch, cut, & weld plants are sorry to be closing,
sorry to unemploy so many.
Your rivers crave the shut-down industry, knowing
the fish have empty, hurt mouths
& the water echoes with their thinking
Pulp & paper
Hydro power
The revolution is over!
There is no more sense in teaching it
in schools.
There is no more sense in teaching your children
to earn money, to desire cars or lawsuits
or expensive ease
Teach them to live on little, to take apart Chryslers
& boil them, to eat their shirt starch,
teach the unemployed to go south
& struggle
with guerrilla armies in *the backyard of America,*
teach them to stay home & stop electing
the CIA.
Sleep, Ontario.
Your industry has leaped out of its cradle &
lunged into its grave, without whining,
except in the Globe & Mail.
Sleep, industry.
Your people will go home & forget,
& wait for the seeds of their lives to burst open,
& speak to the rivers, & fish the brown water-
& leave you to dream alone, Ontario

Five Miles From Detonation

I am one survivor
who would envy the dead
In the midst of nuclear predicament, not
its aftermath–
Our bright lawns strewn with garbage,
so much rot
I hide away from it, my face in my hands, listen
to the motor of wasps lunging
thru the open window, into old cups of
honeyed tea:
The mire of our being connects for one moment.
I hear them plunge in, & the motor
stops,
& the sun goes on as ever before, making its
tracks on linoleum,
& the schools are out for Easter so
the neighbourhood's quiet
& the white seltzer has settled in my glass, undrinkable
The world ends at last for one wasp
as I sit
citizen, imbecile, reading newspapers
Unable to empty my head of predicament:

Third
degree burns, five miles from
the point of detonation.

Camouflage

Trick air, trick
colours, like camouflage, magenta as a
sunset,
scars on the woman's arm
some evenly inflicted
one crooked & hard, a bar fight,
a night in the green corridor of emergency,
not answering questions
Trick air
can't push it away from her
the insects too heavy to fly
the heat unbroken by nightfall
a kiss
The woman opens her legs
& the street looks in
& steps out again, dizzy, with difficulty

A Sporting Life

In a green field on Easter Day,
Jesus rises up among the soccer players;
in the stands people hold
coarse hotdogs, their jobs, celestial navigation, swallowing
the afternoon like an industry.
Jesus begins to speak, about the Liquor Commission,
so many cases of domestic wine;
a famous forward kicks passes around him.
Meanwhile, past the stand, someone thinks about ham
for dinner, garnished with pineapple.
Others sit in a hotel lobby, near the radio,
arguing about lotteries. A sign at their back says:
No noise after this hour.

Around the world, new colloquialisms
are accepted into the language.
I record them with a bad accent,
ill at ease & out of ammo.
Even history books invent fresh causes, sources, continually
reasonable men.
What the facts show at a given hour.
One acts; one acts; never enough
money, too many milkshake cures.

In the green field of afternoon, Jesus.
Risen among the soccer players, finance companies, skewered wieners.
He wants to play, but no one lets him; they call for
evidence, & a set of statutes.
Like refrigerators, ministers, lawyers risen from the universities.
Opposition leaders decrying *the worst government*
in history.
So he turns from the field, Jesus, alone
because the game is not over, & walks
to the Acropol, which he likes; & he sits for hours
beneath its liquor license, the rows of
glasses, the statue
of his blue mother   among the bottles behind the bar

Wedding Party

The women who babysat me in the 1960's,
I wonder who they are
with their bright nails & bubble hair, hardened
They never let us sleep,
blasted the hi-fi so loud into the phone,
one friend to another, yelling above the craze
They had boyfriends with cars, flames scrawled on the metal
Smoked cigarettes on my parents' sofa,
their high shoes & forbidden sweaters, acquiescence
to the male, our hope chest

Before all their weddings I watched them babysit,
the backs of their heads
ducked under the kitchen tap,
washing their hair colour
Their desires sent me out of my mind.
One way or another, the false glow of
the wedding party
a lattice of future need
The possessions divided into gasoline & hairspray
The talk of the *Modern*
With their heads soaked, rubbing red nails on the scalp,
bowed over, silent,
they scared me.
I didn't want to grow to fit their clothes.

Shocks

Like the Indian boy who climbed up into the transformer
& touched the power with his head & shoes,
perfect
except on the inside,
except the scalp burn, the twin burns on his feet

He lay in the hospital for weeks, a vegetable
A place where time stopped & never started,
a shell, a body to trip into
& never grow to adulthood

As my husband did,
poised over the dinner after he tipped it
on the floor, straddling the soft heap
of vegetables
He wavers drunken
Don't touch anything, don't touch me
& I can't answer, just stare at his sad impulse,
shock & hunger

The girl who stuck a spoon into the socket
to find where the TV picture hid
& jolted her arm & neck
A neat bolt of lightning etched in the metal handle
I still have that spoon

How the body's built
to take it, to preserve its likeness,
how it won't remember shock or marriage, & ignores
good proof, sits up at night in its coil of bedding
its hair on end, irresistible

a vegetable with three burns,
smaller than quarters

Safety

Far off in the washroom, the light comes thru, the sound
of him throwing up dinner,
his sickness,
his body so hard it won't digest,
won't welcome food
In the newspaper, a picture of Gilles Villeneuve
in the last second of his life,
his car already demolished,
his body in the air
turned-over
about to slam its bones into the wall
So many kilometres per hour,
with or without the Ferrari.
& the small man in the washroom, who admires
but will not listen
to the fast man who says death is boring.
I can't drive slower, he says.
I drive at my limits, for
the pleasure, purely

& you, in this house, listening to the small man's body
turn over its cylinders,
refusing its food
What part you play here, the pattern,
the man sick with alcohol,
who wants boredom,
who wants to be a dead man in your arms'
bent safety without cure
or derision
the way Villeneuve held his body in the air,
so fast only the camera stopped him

Fusillade

You who claim to pretend nothing
in your neediness.
Your ruse only works for awhile, then ends.
To pretend the heart
a palpable organ, for donation or transplant:
For months, when we walked or drank beer as friends,
or spoke of the fine glow of oranges,
took baths in sunlight, coffee, soft brown bread

I wore your heart in my chest
stubbornly,
pumped my own blood thru it into the air,
my chest delicate, touchy, angered
by the least sentiment.
My chest ate & ate to keep your heart alive,
the famished convert.

The heart is yours, I'll shovel it out of me.
I'd rather depend on my own.
You can't climb in & out of my chest, like a cupboard.
To you, a bowl of saliva!
A lettuce with flames!
No more!

Your heart is not Shakespeare.
I've thrown it out of me.
It's not a grenade!

Amore

The bats rage up & down the fire escape,
knitting new husbands
shadows without doors
white slats thru which the night leaks
Bless us & these thy gifts, my arms ache,
heavy with the weight
of being flesh, & desiring

The bats are my own wish, unhinged,
hitting dark wings against
the railing
their tiny lungs pumping up & down

Or are they my arms, wanting
to go somewhere
afraid to leave me alone,
who will I touch when my time comes?

It's the bats terrify me.
No more radar, no more adrenalin, no more
chance to run up
the fire escape into the building
kissing the cold doorway
My husband who is not my husband
Holding our divorce up
like a key

Public Health

The cold daydreams
that speak to us with their mouths
shut.
They are the thin rook
of a woman dragged
around the walls of her hospital in a chair,
one leg dangles like a crayon
that the sidewalk tears thru.

It is said
the doctor must charge us equally because
he lives by this, his courage,
it is to open up the human skin &
know-
the orange pump, flat machination of breath,
coils of decay that push
the corpuscles forward:
the doctor's courage is in pulling the skin back,
tying off daydreams; & in fingering the cold
muscle, arthritic bone.

This man talks of
the enterprise he finds
in sickness, accidental caresses, the roughed-up
wife, a cirrhosis.
He proclaims his courage, his love, & how
the government wants it, or gives back
too little.
The limbs of the woman mute with anaesthetic.
Pay me, he says.

I'm gonna die, the drunk chokes at
all of us in the liquor line-up, his face battered
open in dispute.
Then laughs, bent over sideways with his 2-dollar bill, ripped trouser,
his left hand pushes his kidneys inward,
rain hits the sidewalk,
the woman is wheeled into surgery two blocks away,
& the cold
daydream shuts its mouth, again

Groceries

Women in their clothes with their hard
hurting sunburnt backs
bent over the groceries
Small figures on the lawn breathing inwardly
The wall sunlit, moss dying off now
Wife in the room waiting for the breakthrough,
the dinner stew
to cook itself better

The woman in the street last night, head beaten with a pipe,
her arms held without direction
The anguish of her mouth's wet noise
inside her brain,
windows empty with her cry
her bare feet corroded
Caught up at last by neighbours, the white ambulant glow
The physical disobedience of the head
jarred by metal
Reaction of the eye & retina to light, to speech
the breakthrough
You aren't wearing shoes, the cop said to her
I got away, she said

As if anyone knows anyone else
As if we can cook anything more
As if we can eat again
without concussion, the thump the pipe makes
in the wall at night,
its groan & shudder
Our bodies bent among the groceries, the room lit up
Deafening

Sowing

Flowers jerk their stems thru the human
skull, its soil that won't speak
is turned over, stubborn.
Dark clots hammered smooth, they cling & scatter.
In the garden, a woman digs
with her back hunched over, the slugs behind her
clamp thin mouths onto the broccoli,
insisting.
She is not sowing, she is crying.
Pardon,

the woman is not sowing she is crying.
She is crying, not sowing.

The flowers she can't grow
cut my tongue with their knives, with their bad surgery,
sour note of whisky in my mouth,
in hers.
I lean out the window, watch the woman:
she amazes me now with her stupid tears,
her vote for the government, her back that she turns
from the slugs, they chew the petals
& beckon her,
they are my own thought, grief inching toward her,
will she hear me moving, look
to the window, see herself there?
It's my lousy grave she's digging, upturning
the huge earth

She wants to sow me in it
with those savage tears: a pale seed, sister & watcher,
her cry upended in my   skull

After All That

for Jennifer MacKenzie, 17 years old

It is the echo of a streetlight in the window,
blue hat of light.
It is the jeopardy makes me write down.
Like Lazarus, I am raised from the dead.
So many times & I never weary.

It is my lungs make me feel this.
The pain the vein spoke when they pushed intravenous into me,
the surprise.
Lazarus too, surprised to have a body
after all that.

You whom we pray to, governors
of the human, of the reported blameless soul.
White-clad people of the hospital.
For *Jennifer MacKenzie,* thrown from a horse

& carried in from air ambulance as I lay there;
unconscious, not breathing on her own;
behind a yellow curtain washed each day & hung between us

You who will never know me, I am sorry.
I'm not blameless.
You whom the medicine won't bring home to your father's sobbing,
I tip my hat of blue light to you, it is silent, a rosary,
it is all I have

Professional Amnesia

He remembers family reunions at Lake Somewhere; each summer
the women running toward the water
laughing,
holding eggs in spoons
In his memory they keep on running,
he can't remember when they reach the water,
their clothes streaked with sand & grass
Or is it
the target shoots he claims had happened,
shooting at old records, ribbons, plastic soldiers
thrown up by the other children,
his cousins, who never grew

In his memory the women are still running,
the water does not rise to meet them,
they run right out of his life
so their names are forgotten
Family names
Family memories, the accusations one parent made
against the other
while he sat outside, his head
pressed against the cold tree that shaded his room

He remembers who stayed away each Christmas but not who came,
who wouldn't cut the turkey,
who stood up in shirt & tie & armbands
& sharpened knives against the steel.
The eaters are forgotten, the celebrations spontaneous
combustions;
when he speaks of family
the women are running out of it, into a summer lake of air

Dawn Of The Unwed

Enough of secret wedded bliss!
My glands have stopped their wailing,
insistent as sirens, traffic pulled to the curb
as my desire flashed, high speed
passage of blue
When I look at my stereo it starts up
crazily, the mat under the record
spinning
Enough of this static.
I'm tired of your body coming over to mine
in its taxi & raincloud,
your cigarette smoke reeling down the wall,
tonight's newspaper unread
I'm sick of shaking your sad stains
out of the bedsheets,
sick of putting your sperm in me like money!
Or: I'm not sick, I'm happy.

To be free of you,
to dream,
to carry my own desire in me,
broken open, unwed, crow black, a drowned lake,
ocean-swell of gloom

Hoe

Like the cowboy in the western film hoeing
a cabbage row, horizon of bleak fields at his back
& him inside the garden fence,
gently working the blade

I am misplaced in my own life, passing
this time only,
to look but not touch

When I see you in the street downtown
I can't go where I'm going,
we're both going to the same place
So I turn away

Pretend I wasn't going there, pretend
I didn't want a beer
Or that I was just leaving, a bit tipsy into
the street, a raw field

I am commencing just now
to hoe

Speaking in Tongues

Private Windows

They make you cross their bridges when you come to them,
make you shut your eyes on
a tremor of skin
Make you reach out   & not touch them,
make you hold your storm until the wish subsides
You burn on
coffee in the late night of their absence,
you are celibate until you see them,
obsessed of their arms, no–
One arm   & their kisses, warm, urgent, possessing you

Impossible;
to know them so easily
To touch them without knowing them
To embrace them without them
knowing you
These Halifax women, so calm
when faced with your calm exterior,
they jump out of private windows, into each other's arms

Sitting Inside Talking

They drag up the problems of twenty years.
They know what so-&-so did, & etcetera.
Their fists bang up & down on the table,
obeying gravity,
the wine spills. Gullets.
The intestinal system of the gull, & then some.
The stomachs & birds!

Their digressions are out on the porch
wearing peaked tweed hats, teetering
on the stairs.
Will they ever go home!
Their potatoes are just potatoes.

& sometimes, their potatoes are
committees.
Their reading material is inside
the slats of blinds, &
everything between,
every bit of scenery.
The alps & the boulevard, the kid running down 10th
with a garden rake,
me on my bicycle yesterday,

the news.
They are professional neighbours.
I am finished drinking with them this time for
good.
I am finished with their description,
& the chapters, & the subject hats they wear
when they are cheating,
& the gulls they have declared!

Vision Of A Woman Hit By A Bird

The flutter in my blood after the bird hit, as if
I would fall too,
head-on
into my throat, a soft body shaking its wings
& fallen
past me, the shock of it, its fury

at my chest unseen,
as if the bird had nested in me, that quickly.

Always now I am the woman hit by a bird.
I stand without emblem & defer
to my companions, their maleness & femininity,
their dress is a strangeness without purity;
I can't show them
my memory of the path under the trees
where I ran & was hit by the bird,
its brown eye, sincerely,
the blurred flight too late to stop
hitting my neck, then diving unhurt past me

Its mark is on my skin, a thin scrawl
invisible to medicine,
the bird's look in me, a hole,
sensible
Now I see the world thru my chest without asking,
as if I had the bird's eyes & bone flotation,
the earth's axis tipped,
spun away from the humans with their doctors' faces

The bird's stain I bandage on me,
heroically,
not like an emblem,
as if it were still the size & weight of a bird,
transubstantial,
its body on my throat with a flutter,
inexcusable surely,
my temperature at long last,
my melting point

Secret Kisses

It's now that our kisses don't seem real.
It's because they don't happen in real places,
but in the rough nerve of alcohol,
the rough sniper of clothing, caught in the wall's shadow,
fed by wine.
& night,
& the stars' incense falling
into our bare arms' reach
Oh ache, I love you
Oh alphabet, your secret nest is harboured in my tongue
Oh agony released in dreams, my body
craves you

As if it were nature
I could kiss any *man* & pretend it's you-
The world would stay in its brown corridors
& not care!
I want an age   where I can turn my neck
& kiss you at dinner
among real roast beef & oranges,
real salads,
our co-workers watching,
I want to pull your head close with my fingers,
I want to be clumsy,
I want my lips to feel kissed by you,
to feel natural
& not   so crooked or so rare

Spirit-Catcher

What I am is never clear, is the heart
lonely, is a word, dusk,
bed-eaten
Love, I am the veined-blue iris in your hand
when you clench fists
breaking over nothing
I'm the dust during years of renovation, the pulse
of cats
The disturbance of light, the still loaf of rye
The shudder, ecstasy you bring me
as if it were grace, or usual

My body is the thing you see that's slowly
dying,
the first click of the phone
before a ringing
It won't focus cleanly in the hemisphere we're in

where women are hungry & the dead are pushed full of bread
& sewn
An excess in the mouths of presidents
who talk of the nation's *sanctity,* the right to *pray*
of which there is none
We pray without right, as we must

just as I drink, to get out of my body,
out of the light's psychic noise on my skin
It's said the spirit leaves us thru the mouth, which
is why I speak to you
The maps of my body fail me, a sheer bulk
stopping transmission
closing shop
My silence, deaf as radar

Quebec Street At 1AM

There is the ragged man bowed,
the dark trees, there are
many murderers, some
who murdered without speaking, without saying
sorry,
as their knives wore down the food.
There are walls of churches &
the grocery still open,
sells its milk at this hour.

There is the shot from the gun
that the blind man takes
softly in his mouth, like communion,
its bullet hurts no one who would live.
There are letters in the mailbox that murmur
all night to each other,
trying to find why they say their messages,
the same old things.
Even the payphone is busy, weighing its dimes.
At night on my street there is one
of everything,
& when the one meets the one,
they embrace each other, knowing darkly
where their passion is,
where their tongues can meet & enter

&, even if they hear the gunshot
the passersby will not look around

Paleohora Wind

The visible house of magic, a tree shorn by wind,
dusk,
the house light grows across our fingers,
lighting our wine
On the balcony where we sit among oranges,
above the washed heads & the olives,
the woman who scolds the goat & chicken,
to whom the goat & chicken listen,
she brings their corn &
sticks of food

The barber opens his shop below & sees first
his face in the mirror
& bows to his features
then closes
Men of the village unshaven at his door

The barber gone
another orange
another harvest of olives
the goats & their hot bellies lying down
Wind tearing the tree, pushing café chairs over,
scraping the wood

The magic visible, a drink of light
wine hurting the chest,
to be here gladly, in our old eyes of the wheaten prairie,
the white forehead & salty fingers,
drunk with clarity
in our lifetimes,
breathing thru our *stoma*, our *dentia*, & skin

Angelus Domini

To say *prophecy*, to say *reason*
& fight out
the length between them,
a broken board for a measure, for an audience
a girl in the fast-food apron, reading a comic on the lawn.
The stale houses of memory shut their doors,
sweepings on the doorstep.
You're swept away by the tide of cars
passing red lights into infinity.
The radio brings back
rock & roll of the sixties,
you turn it up,
curious,
wondering where you stand in this.
It is what you remember.
It is all.
It is all a noise.
It is all over.
The young are
younger than you.
The sum total of reason has not changed
one bit.
& the sum of prophecy:
the time you've had & wasted, an Incarnation
you couldn't quite manage, a light-
space scarcely open
in the road between the pell-mell cars

The Words Mean What We Say, We Say

This is a fear of no vocabulary
a world where things are speeches
where a car is a whole book
aluminum siding a framework
for history
where roses are grown to mean love, to sell love
where silence is an auto-da-fé

This is a fear of no word ever
of no word that does not
mean an object
a fear of microphones implanted
of words transmitted over distance
translation that talks of

boundaries, disputes over ideology,
as if a belief is protected
the more guns you sell
the more disenfranchised
the more advisors sent to administer foreign justice
language flushing out the guerrillas
Hollywood triumph & news

The power of speech empties our mouths
Even the heretic in his fiery skull
can't name the word
harsh as the presence we attend to
Its stutter, in him, is all we are,
to speak of

Speaking In Tongues

Someday I'll show you where I stood,
the year the flames were tongues,
our idiot foreheads
speaking in tongues, torches, singing, tongues of children
8 years old in winter clothing, testing the harshness
of cold steel
Lick the fence, my head dared
& my tongue froze sudden to the metal links
of the fence between two schools
Unwise child in a field of snow,
in a city of backyards & bouffant hair,
the death of presidents on TV,
the silence of women everywhere

But frightened cold, stuck to the fence,
my tears ran hard in the lonely hub of Calgary,
which was nowhere,
my friends gone into school
the fence not as high as I imagine
the snow more trampled
The Baptist who came out in shirtsleeves from the other school
who poured sweet coffee on my tongue to free it,
my body displaced from dreaming
his arms white with cold
Sometime I'll show you how he warmed me, in the empty snow,
the coffee spilled between us,
at the chain-link fence where it clove the air in two,
where my life touched & untouched,
a shy flame
not yet capable of speaking

Tropic Line

The northern pike, blinded, its mouth open in the hook's pull
upward from the water, reverse gravity
My brother's hand holding the pike's body,
long & more muscled than his arm,
lifting it:

My brother in the jacket too small for his age,
its green quilt unravelling
around him, unweaving his body into the cold March
air, the snow receded but not gone,
the river's effluent opening

Our hands nearly solid with cold, gloveless,
immobile
Out on the river ice, hearing it explode
beneath us like a rifle
Deep noise of the hemisphere, turning toward the sun

What we would do, to go out with the narrow rods
like saplings, fibreglass, the crude reels,
cheapest ever made,
we would hike behind the river houses, the winter unchanged
Sun risen just past the Tropic of Cancer

To rub our hands & feel ice crack inside the fingers,
not like rifles,
like meat slightly frozen
Billy still holding up the pike, stubborn,
bright fish dripping water

Fish we hurt in the sole motion our hands were capable
before we threw it back
into water that would freeze us if we fell
Not knowing how the pike had come where we were fishing,
crazed & lonely, searching its prey

How it saw our pattern of light on the river surface,
our shadows & colours, the last it saw
Blind with cold we blinded it with ice shards,
& returned it, & ourselves, our arms & hands raised
like rifles, triumphant
The sun at our backs too cold to kill us,
pushing north over the tropic line

Neighbours

They are in the street boiling the sweat out
of their clothes
In their houses scraping paint off the door
to eat it as a meal
They are in the basement sleeping at work-benches
after the tools are sold
They fidget
Social workers come in & out of their doors
Their drawings are suspect
& their lists of groceries
too much love & insufficient macaroni
what is this

Do they think they can get away
Do they think *steal*, do they know the sad night
of hunger after the children are fed
Do they dream of jobs

They are the neighbours
Hello my neighbours
In this age there are more of us than there are soldiers
Still, if we cry out our sadness & break the government
will it turn us into salt
or food

Eight Ways Of Going To Trial

With anaesthetic for the lungs.
With one book memorized perfectly, sentence
character & typeface, shape of
the O's,
width of margins, stippled surface of the page:
to remember when the lights are down.
With belief in due process.
With the address of the RCMP, round mark
on your head where the gun was pushed,
& on the other side,
the highway.
All this talk of left & right brain.

With disbelief in the state.
With eighteen months in custody & no bail
& a precise image of the physical layout of a court.
With small maps drawn on banana stickers.

With recuperative abilities.
Without looking, with a slate concealed
in the sinews of the neck
to fill up over & over

& wipe clean.

Philosophy Of Language

A certain level of noise, the ear's false anguish, period.
She is reading a book, to herself, the
noise of this.
Huge rustling shakes the trees.
The windows fall open & lunge three stories downward
in a pirouette, ready for suicide.
A man stands up before her,
for all his height he is no taller than her shoe.
It is the inventor of the hinge.
He wants her to praise him
for inventing it.
When she leans forward the noise of the book
blows him over.

He wants her to love him, that's all.
But he shuts her out, waving the god-damn
almighty
root of language.
For all his bellow, he is no more agile
than a verb.
For all his pirouette, he is no regeneration.
He is no earth & no simile.
When she leans her woman-being toward him, he is
no name.
She is her simple rustling, shakes him, utterly,
without syndical perfection,
without period

Like The Rain
for G.S.

Sometimes everything smells like the rain.
Sometimes my problems smell like the rain,
small droplets on the far side
of glass, or
Soaking into the clothes, shoulders downward.

Try taking a nose dive into reality, come up
gasping & tell me what it is, what
makes you lunge
in & thru my kisses

Hey when I get up so fast in the morning,
do you think it's hard?
Are any of these things hard?

Are kisses   hard?

Some days the rain is cleaning the whole city,
water eventually wears away stone, they say,
if it persists.

The country smells like the country.
Sometimes I can only compare things to themselves.
How can I break free of this?

& how the rain *sounds,* how about that, too?

3000 miles of country, between us, in a few days
I'll be that far.

Are we satellites?
Are voices satellites?

Is the rain?

Idiom Birds

The cars in the shut lot are burning their doors.
Sandwiches unravel their tongues,
sucking the mouth.
All the idioms have been written out.
Modernity is a hard beak, to cherish.
Unwrite idiom.
Tip over idiom, tailless haunted bird,
stable currency,
that which speaks,
that which wanders, cloud with trousers,
yo-yo,
brink, my sad revolver, my door.

Open up or be stolen, passing sentence
in the getaway car,
gunning its verbs like a motor.
Unseal.
Unrip & sew, bluster, speak, who listens, who hears
or writes
unless I'm smirking, pulling phrase
out of the cupboards, idiom birds
Come on, birds
trying to dance their bone skulls
on the window
hard syllables named Apollinaire, their guns
thrown in the gas tank,
trapped birds,
my idiom, soft idiom, tastes like hay

Some Of The Women

Some of the women I know look like the men I imagine.
Some of the women I know are
wearing blue silk softly this year.
Some of the men I know look like, crazily, & look away.

At the side door, the man with light shirt
& upturned collar leans forward,
holding his hand out from his body,
he points it toward the door jamb & turns

He lifts one arm, no one is watching, before he enters
he touches the future, like silver, like a blade,
a small cut in the sky close to his fingers,
like computer satellite

Some of the women I know are wearing dresses
with prints of sailing boats on blue
& pants underneath that.
Some of the women I know are dancing, I know

they are still dancing, the light flashed
on their front & sides makes their bodies
jump jaggedly in the air,
never touching the dance floor

ever again.
I want the men I know to look like women.
I want the men I know to stop imitating us & be someone.
I want the men I know to stop inventing.

As if you can lie about your dreams

Thaw

Including Myself

Everybody who has lived in Vancouver, ever.
Everybody who has lived in Vancouver
for ten years.
Everybody who has had a job, a jacket, drink
when they need it, at a price
they can afford.
In ten years there is no molecule in the body
that is the same.
What identity is, has been overworked
in these pages.

The small snow under the birch near Morley
Alberta.
How this is a trick to say
small snow.
My brother fumbling with his camera & frowning,
checked shirt & muddy boots,
standing in the highway ditch under the birches,
black cloud over him.

In ten years my brother came to see me in Vancouver
three times.
On the average, once every three years,
with one year over.
We pounded our feet on the floor
singing London Homesick Blues till the woman
from downstairs came up to remind us
her husband was dying of cancer
& did not want to hear our feet or
London Homesick Blues.
Whatever.

None of the molecules are the same in their bodies either.

My brother is in Toronto on the top floor of
a house, going to school.
When he was in Morley he was a groundskeeper.
Now just out his kitchen window is a small
tin screaming-porch.
Who knows who started this name but this is
what it is called.
It leads nowhere. You can only scream from it.

Everybody who has lived in a Canadian City, including
myself.
In ten years none of the molecules of our bodies
will be the same as now.
We should get to know each other
quickly.
We should rejoice.
We should walk into the street or onto the screaming-porches,
before we are too
different or too changed,
& call out, offering each other
our future absence, our private & immoderate discourse,
the place where we are hoarding
memory, & the small snow

Visible Ordination

Those of us who fear the dancers,
the placement of mint
over the heart
The scent of the hands after the bread is made
Those who see the clay in bricks
who see bricks in hillsides
& mint in the far hill

We, yes, who hear the mothers speaking to their children,
& the fathers to their fathers' graves,
who crave a space with no America
so that we can rest
We for whom the statue of Liberty faces inward
& claps

Our answer is the ducks calling in the rocks,
is the chicken walking behind a sweater,
is human always,
agape & easily entered,
the letter on the inside of a host of bread

Those of us who fear the dancers
know the dance is a bright window
of oxygen in the head
We who look out the window
sadly
see the dancers eat before they know they will be dancing,
on the ocean terrace of the tavern,
salt blown on their shoulders,
beneath the cedars
with their white, white inner wine

Five Highways

So much is not happiness, not
a possible world, not visible
Look at my hands, the woman on the porch says
holding her palms outward, pale hands
like anybody's, no different
the field outside them green & empty
the woman reaching

& me embarrassed, unable to tell,
it's only
the place where her arms end,
& split into the five pieces,
the five unwritten sequences,
the five skies

that push away the air into its colours

But I peer into her skin, the lines familiar,
there's nothing there, I say
but she continues to insist on me,
the porch & hayfield,
dusk just ending
Because she can't feel anything more,
not even the usual sadness of the hands
their fine & usual tensity
the space where her body won't be reprieved,
or forgive

Her hands strain, atomic in desire,
her proof of physicality,
her resemblance purely
In the porch-lit darkness
her photograph & five highways,
the soft grip of the digits on her name

Riding Blind

The spaces we don't see, that
time lets into us.
Between our fingers, where we touched each other,
or between the breast bone   & the skin,
a small bubble of light, pried open

It reflects our faces, reversed & upended, pale
Along the corridors, the space unseen
between   the arm & the chest,
the arm & the chest's blue jacket,
between the hand & the thigh

The small, identified clearance
between the eye & the optic medicine, correction of sight
Between the instep & the shoe
Whole sentences, safe in the arch under the foot
& not stepped on

Space between the legs, standing.
Space, always
between one & the other thigh, between one rib & another,
between the twist of muscles,
between the two adult bones of the leg

The spaces we don't see, inside us
when we ride   the way we came at dusk
on unlit bicycles, lunging our legs on the grey pedals,
thinking of the brakes,
will they work   in the dark, wet distance

we are keeping now
between our machines

Fentiman Avenue

The roses are out along Fentiman Avenue.
I get up out of my chair & ask
my father if there were roses.
I cross out the line.
The roses are out in the gardens along Fentiman Avenue.
I am out looking for the three Billys.
One of them grew up to be
my Dad, but I am not looking for my father.
The roses are out in the soft dirt of Fentiman Avenue.
The three Billys are in their ripped t-shirts
in the shade, if possible.
The houses are full of dust & cat hair, &
the dogs are ornery.
There was Billy Mouré, Billy Hall, & Billy Moberg.
The roses are out along Fentiman Avenue.
I am not sure if there were
ever roses.
I was eight years old when my father showed me
the house on Fentiman for the first
& last time.
I get up out of the chair & go to the window.
My father is walking up & down Fentiman Avenue.
I know this is true.
He is one of the three Billys.
It happens to be August.
In the picture there are roses.
I cross out the line.

Lions

It's all new.
We are angels splitting theological hairs
or party jokes, or just
a piece of cake with jam in the middle,
the way my mother made it for our birthdays,
Ken's birthday when he got the hamster,
that died after biting Steve Groszko.
We could see Steve's garage from our house, & his new fence.
From our kitchen window where the light came
thru green ruffled curtains
my mother sewed after the night classes.
Under the kitchen table where I lay while my father
kicked out at me, yelling
Get up! No one is hurting you!
Later, Steve Groszko died of cancer.
He never did drink anything at the neighbourhood
Christmas parties.
That's the kind of man a family wants, my mother said.
We listened gravely, drinking up the rum
in our root beer & fighting each other
in the basement.
That was later.
We felt sorry for the rest of the Groszkos.
Or I felt sorry.

When I think of it, I can still see his garage.
Between it & his house, a small space
where you could see the park paid by the Altadore Lions.
I saw my brother out there once, the day the dog
got run over by a bread truck.
Between the houses, he was so small, screaming.
You could hear him in our kitchen over a block away.
That's the kind of man a family wants, my mother said.
He finished the new fence before he died.
How do they get enough to eat, I wondered.
There's some kind of pension, she said.
My brother was outside screaming.
Steve was one of the Lions.
The space between the houses was so small.

Like This One

There are hours & hours of small
collapses
like this one, coming out of the house
with a jacket & toque on, late fall, the cigarette cutting
the mouth's edge, open,
open up,
bedevil memory.
Any of this could have been, five years ago.
Young, then.
Looking for your friends on the railway, or just
pretending, who you are waiting for,
who will walk in,
who you will buy the drink for.
Your coat crumpled on the chair beside you,
your back bent over, the lights of the place
reflected in the lines of glasses,
mirrored shelves,
mechanical perfection & noise
Or your neighbours with their pushpins, at night
they burrow into your walls
& look in
pointedly
Your hand caressing you, stops startled & looks up
& the loud crash of guitar music
you're used to, this is the way you grew up lonely
& fell into the hours
Street-wise, savvy, where you live now,
the neighbourhood of
funerals & beggars, rolled up for winter in the trees

Thaw

Wherever you go it's as if
you'd come out of the cold at Broadview
your hands don't match
They're frozen into the doorhandles
Still your ears are singing,
it's somebody's birthday, more rum
& coca-cola,
more ice blown by the door
so hard your lungs are crusted

Your divorce just repeats itself
up & down the wall,
silly
you can laugh now, everybody does it,
the cake's cut into squares as if it's a wedding,
every time the door is opened
the bar gets richer, but for you
it's Broadview,
it's the prairie at 40 below, the wind 150
freezes your eyelids to the glass
You're on a train & the passengers are in danger
of freezing,
you tell them to stay under blankets & embrace

Every street sign says it's Broadview,
the light at the end of the bar
is the first light of Broadview,
your crippled train makes it into town to thaw,
the feet torn off your legs without feeling
So somebody turned on the ice,
filled your boots & left them like buckets
It's a play you'll never get used to,
as if you were thawed out of steam pipes no matter
what house you're in, the people talk
idiocy while the wind-chill rises,
your snowy boots sent alone to warn them,
drifted out of kilter, smashed on whisky, tipped over
crying outside the doors

Doe-Face

Soft fur of her doe-face in the snow below the rails
Brown on brown body, warm-blooded, still
The cow elk hears the ticking of
her hunger
The animals of prey do not attack her
Know she will die here & they will eat from her
Easy meat
Hit by the passenger train, skidded down
the snow slope into silence
Wild she gazes, soft ears spread out, supplicant among trees
her body alert as the trains speed above
Their track so civilized & named
A siding called Palliser, below it
the elk waits, grass torn from beneath the snow
as far as she could nuzzle,
unable to stand
Already she does not know what her life was, she
becomes the snow, lain in trees under the mountain

It's our emotion, not hers
She doesn't feel the heart welling up
or know she waits to die
That's just us, projecting our own incapacity,
her body still alive
suffering pain without cry or madness
She looks up, her long ears & animal intensity,
legs folded under her,
a brown patch in the white sentence
She watches our train pass,
without coming down from our dangerous track
to know & rescue her from hunger
To touch her
Bringing in our arms, like game wardens,
a warm shot for her

How I Will Look At You

If light has a certain texture, if you can
weave it in & out of our warm skins
& pull us together,
two figures drowning in a building, the colour,
what it would be
how they would find us
Today Princess Grace of Monaco died,
brain hemorrhage after a car accident.
& the lost family was found in unmarked territory,
burned up, six bones inside their car.
Light, handfuls of light
woven together, the fabric of identity,
I with you,
identify me, touch me, stubborn, my hands

Last night I dreamed I kissed you finally,
unasked for, my desire clumsy,
your skin worn & startling
I held you with my hands to kiss you
& you answered, then pushed me away

So I woke, it was 5am,
your kiss had lifted the light out of my room
out of the sky
into my body, charged with the taut thread
I stole from you, happily
I got up then, dressed & worked alone
the light burned
between my lips
& melted, & turned to daylight, the way
I will look at you this morning,
if I see you, how they will find us,
if you let me be

Geese

for Lorna Crozier

Our wish for the geese is that they will be known as swans,
in their lifetimes
& For the swans
that their breath will be of geese
that their god-eyes will see heaven in the slough
& grass sticking out of it in hurried clumps like hair

Our wish for sparrows is that they will grow up to be geese.
Our wish that chickadees will qualify
as the national bird of Ontario.
In their lifetimes.
Our wish is that geese will carry a small round portion of blue
                                        in their soft chests
                                        as they fly.
It is geese that are our characteristic, geese
who have taught us citrus & the shore.
Geese are our ambassadors more so than Air Canada,
they nest at home.
Geese are free.
Geese let goddesses lie beside them
without claiming they sprung them from their heads.
Geese have a sense of the ludicrous.
Swans are only interesting as ideas
            arranged certainly.
Swans are less heady than the weather.
Geese have direction.
Geese bring the morning with a raucous noise.
When geese see the world go up they will go up with it,
still lifting the blanket of the slough.

Bends

What the heart is is not enough.
That I can open it &
let you enter
an ocean so dense
you'll get the bends if you surface.
That you will be open to the love of every being:
I crave this,
it makes me possible, anarchic, calling
your attention,
your fingers' madness on my ear or soft neck,
the light on each side of your face, altered
as you speak to me

Oh speak to me
I have a friend who says the heart's
a shovel, do you believe this?
My heart is a wild muscle, that's all,
open as the ocean
at the end of the railway,
a cross-country line pulled by four engines

Whatever it is I don't care, it is not enough
unless you see it
unless I can make you
embrace & breathe it, its light that knows you,
unless you cry out in it, & swim

Paradisiacal Vallejo

He died of the war before it came,
his eye too hurt by pardons,
the talk of armed men brave before dying

Sometimes I am only a small wound,
a small hole in the skull
thru which brilliant light leaks,
a flaw betraying paradise.
The paradise in me that I mistake for loneliness
& tramp around it, hunched over like bears.
For spite!

What gamble he played, his hair combed freely
to the point of a flame,
his boots studded with worship,
he stood in the noise of red earth furrowed
until he died of growing

He was a poet that paradise leaked thru,
that shone thru his skull's plate
before I was born,
before any Franco, any penalties, or cure

& paradise leaked out of both of us
in the boom of a million guns, in sonar, in
blips or ack-ack, in tin mines, in Cruise
& won't come back ever
Yet waits in us like bears,
so faithful: his photograph bowed at the road-side,
this hard poem

Cherish

for Libby Scheier

The expression of longing,
in & among
the collapse of social systems,
among facts such as fish see colour;
in a room where light cannot enter the high window,
where mugs are empty of coffee & contain
so many ounces of the room's air,

in the room where air dips close
between the arms,
where women are not forgetful any longer
but tell their whole stories
& fear their body's message,
being alone

The essential barrier
The unknown way to cherish aloneness
& dispel it as a waste
The cups are empty on the floor all night long,
the plates have tipped their crumbs into the paper,
the paper has lain stubbornly unread
until its news is no more sensible,

until Salvador is liberated or invaded,
the fish are suffocating in their own waters,
the future has occurred & not been announced yet
Women
in the ease of their voices' murmur,
able to express but not dispel
anything
To talk without loneliness
because it has been acknowledged & achieved
in our own bodies
Because here the cups are full of the noise
of our laughter,
because no touch is the answer & we know it giddily
& The longing for it
purely
makes us full

Domestic Fuel

Jump Over The Gate

I come home &
tell my mother I grew up.
I grew up! I say, & hug her.
Isn't it amazing! she says.
I go outside & open & slam
the door of the old refrigerator on the patio.
Our refrigerator!
Its round back like asthma, silent now;
a toque of snow over it.
Where did you come from? my mother says when I'm in.
I lay my mitts like two pages on the floor,
my boots dripping muddy smiles of water.
You! I say.

& she laughs. She's sitting at a high stool,
higher than the kitchen table,
paring an old soft cheese into a bowl.
I dip my hand in to taste.
It's good, I say.
Eat it on crackers! says my mother.

It bugs her most when I lean out the screen door
to call the dog out of the snow. Trix! I yell.
Puppy! I yell.
The dog is dead! my mother cries to me, but
I know she's still there in the yard.
Trix! I yell. We're going shopping!
Mom, I'm bringing the dog, I shout back to her.
Now the inside air is out, & vice versa,
it's cold.
Go ahead if that's what you like,
my mother sighs.
There should be a dog! I think.

Trix is with me & I let her run fast
& dip her head into the snow,
grabbing a big mouthful. She lopes ahead &
waits for me at the corners.
Cross! I yell.
& on the way back, I think:
if Trix were here she'd carry the package.
She liked to carry the package.
Trix! I yell for good measure.
Puppy! I yell for good measure.
When I get home, we both
jump over the gate.

You're back! my mother says.
There's really no Trix, I tell her;
& pass her the package, my boots scuffed with wet snow,
& pull the wool of my toque off my head.

I call her because I feel like it! I tell my mother.
I know! she says.
I know!

Rye & Pickerel

We're all of us looking older.
After augering thru, oh, three & a half feet of ice,
our overcoats hunched up & waiting for pickerel,
the seven layers of sleep
our lines caught in the lake water
Bottle of rye whisky handed between us, taste
of camp fire & old salt, of fry pans, of the soft
gut flung into the snow
hiss of the Coleman's white gas
cold silvery fishes, lake-echo pulled up

After breakfast, rye & pickerel, car driven off the lake
to the road, frozen muskeg, sun up
The grit & holler of our bodies.
Don't kid yourself.
We're looking older.
We talk about chain-saw accidents, or the fish last winter.
We fall out of the car like inheritors
of another species.
The pickerel stare at us, deafened, light-headed, their
bungled names we don't know,
a city under the ice.
We're too far gone to imagine

At Night

At night, we embrace each other's clothes & hope to find us,
if anyone,
ourselves. Arms' length.
Using the stories.
Once, we say:
when I was walking back after the film, the dusk
pressed flat on the curve of the Hydro building,
the whole force of the sky
compressed in front of me
& Later, a man on the corner wearing one sheet of paper
on his head, it blew off & he picked it from the road
& replaced it, repeating everything
His gesture

How we are virtually imprisoned
one step out of our bodies, our sweaters
wrapping thin air.
The violence inside families.
The heart's small noise, what is it, incurable,
drives us.
Being unable to compare,
this is madness:
shunning comparison.
The heart's noise is a cool urge to metaphor.

Bless us & these thy gifts, heavy
with the weight of desiring.

Watching Newsreels At The Farm *or*
Beirut From Westerose

The pig eating out of the trough of a
man's head
A pig eating its master
A journalist drinking coffee, mortar
fallen at her door, she keeps
writing
The city is calm tonight
A salesman sells films, the injured smoke
their cigarettes
A tree rises toward the hill
Guns & belts
of cartridge-
shells
Seashells
Powder, metal casings, noun, noun,
death
In the sky, red with the smoke of buildings
afire in the north
Verb, verb   says the sky
Step out of the farmhouse to smell it, forest fire at Loon Lake
Too far for meaning
Why keep
writing
You're safe here

Domestic Fuel

Our argument at barbecues, summer, when to
turn the steaks over,
who dumped the salad in the lawn, who picked
ants out of the mayonnaise.
We are all bleak, bleak beings,
when the charcoal goes out, we don't see it, we eat
raw meat, our stereo speakers rumble,
the neighbour mows a safety strip across the lawn
& we argue

Who did what,
who was responsible, exactly,
who burnt dinner & the peonies with the firestarter
last year,
throwing gasoline on the barbecue
& lighting his arm on fire, no–
your arm, angry
lit up with the flame's noise
& I jumped on you, put it out with embraces,
pushed you into the garden,
silent, without hunger,
worn out of domestic fuel

Horse Chestnuts

They are fierce brains with
rosewood handles.
We warmed them in our jacket pockets & peeled off the rosewood
over beer in the New West pub,
tearing it slowly with our fingers, unlocking
our deftness & wonder, & inside the rosewood:
the shrunken contours of the brain.

They're poisonous, the woman in the food store says.
You can see her leg tattoos where her socks end.
Blue Maori whirls.

Now on the street when the boy with the gel hair says
grab a brain
we grab it & show him, laughing.

In the restaurant, we flash the brains like credentials.
Already they are stained from the air.
We've brought our brains, we say, cupping our hands
to the hostess,
& are seated, far from the others,
& take out two birthday candles & light them in the ashtray,

balancing our brains on the glass edges, to see.

Remembering Sheep

I remember enough sheep!
Already the sheep of my childhood are waking,
sheep of my sweater,
sheep of the inside of my shoe.
The noise of sheep, head-sheep, wild
under the pillow, sheep of the night's sickness,
shallow wool of the lungs
Sheep of my collar in school, washed & fastened, the blood
tick louder than the chalk of teachers

Voice of sheep!
Sheep, I tell you! Sheep.
Sheep knitted into undershirt & blanket,
cut into skin against mountain winter,
sheep-furnace, fierce as coal.
Sheep I ate for my supper, of my stomach,
of my bones.
Fuel of sheep!
Fertilizer & yoghurt!
Sheep of Christ, Lamb of lambs!

Sheep of my age & habit; adult, I am wearing
more sheep, older,
the pain I feel in me is sheep,
is the noise *sheep* on the tongue,
singular or plural,
the ewe of my body,
ewe of my self-reference,
ram of Sundays, ram of my eye, host of hosts,
ram of my birth in Aries,
my name

Reputation of sheep, wool makers, fuckers of shepherds!

Now,
sheep of my travels, tied under grey olive branches,
heavy, the colour of soil, stands
under centuries of olives, centuries of foot & patience,
sheep I have come to
out of sheepness, shared sheepness,
sheep of my back & eyesight,
I see where it is looking:
a small hill & pail of lightest water

More & more I am like this, ever more
sheep, sheepishly, my head narrow & pointed forward,
with the stubbornness of animals,
the short rope of my own wool I am tied to,
under the olive,
standing, freely

Adoration

Tonight I am not myself
The Virgin Mary is stepping off the front porch
into the plum tree,
her shoulders framed by hair,
lit by a long glow from the archway
Silently she descends, her eyes
are blindness & cannot be received by radio
& cannot beckon
I am not myself
The mass murderer is outside raking dirty cobbles
into the lawn, preparation for spring
& renewal
The rain soaks us gently with its dark thimbles,
reflection of the Virgin's sore birth-
I falter, can't remember
the latin prayer, the worship,
the Virgin with her rolled skirt behind the sweet-pea trellis,
waiting as the storm encloses,
I adore you, an adoration, a memory:
my own mother on a back porch in Calgary in 1950,
shaking out bedding
5 years before I was able, before I craved her
skin's warmth, & was born

West

As if prairie is, the
dry yellow grass cut by gravel, roads of industry,
asphalt, hot noise of flies in the ditch
Crickets in summer, the edge of Wetaskiwin Alberta
coming into town, car heat trapped
by the roof & windows, the woman
trapped by her shirt & bare legs, the field's green
whisper

How in my body, resting
in the night's silence of Montréal,
the west in me,
chart & bearing, grass in my voice as I am speaking,
its intonation,
my distance from it,
la culture ou l'inculture
the hot air cooling finally in me
rough slam of the pick-up door
The clicking of an engine as it cools,
the vehicle empty

in Wetaskiwin, outside the Co-op, it is
the failure of consumption
to mean anything,
the pride which is a road flat upon the prairie
between post offices, *Wetaskiwin, Falun, Ma-Me-O*
where our memory is no older
than the grasses, crickets deafening the soft ditches,
men & women in the roles of small-town painfulness
& rocky soil
Pulling the cut truck of barley down the road with
farm machinery,
#3 Damp if the elevator takes it,
this western,
this goddamn music on the radio, inside my body,
visible if I speak or not,
wherever I am sleeping

Glow

Sitting in the old glow of summer, elbows
hunched over knees,
a bone marker in the green yard, clothed:
In the sun the body gives up its drugs
for stories.
The trees have run to the edge of the clearing, trampling their leaves.
They wait, tipped over, burnished, alive.

In the kitchen the kettle has boiled dry, the children lance long cries
into the yard.
Still the body sits, empty, staring dull eyes at the wood's edge.

Far away the branches tremble, tear their heart-
beat thru the air.
Desire creeps back to the body like a dog.
Children run from the house, the door bangs, somewhere
a key clicks in the ignition of a car.
Even the children, like trees, stand back from the body,
which hunches silently.
It touches their shadows with its hand.
Then stands up, a bone marker facing the yard.
"*Once*," the body begins, talking softly, raising & lowering its
arms, white semaphor, its voice bending over & over,
pushes the years down.

Its life has been the death of many, today the body knows
what the pain was,
& how much it cost, & how many others
broke down crying & admitted everything: subversion, forbidden papers,
the knives.
The body looks around, the children play quietly away from it,
when it gets old, it knows they will not come.
It dreams of the last days it will spend, in bed,
stuck with tubing, the voices loud.

Even now the body knows, a bone marker in the glow of summer,
the trees halted impossibly   out of reach,
the children   impossibly   far & immune to calling
The body   already wise   stands & falters in need of its drug

Gills

The seven kinds of pain of which we are speaking.
The small bones of the fish peeled up
& outward from the eaten body,
a cage on which our sight is fixed,
seeing the fish
jump out of the light blue chop
of water.
Alone, the pain is, pulling
the bent hook out of the fish's lip,
the fish struggling its smooth muscle.
Or the girl who waded up to her boot tops
in an icy current, shooting the fish
with a .22, or just
kicking it upward, out of the water.

The pain from which we speak, we speak
to pull the hook
of our words thru the other's lip, nearest the bone,
tearing it, saving the hook.
I remember Dogpound Creek on the neighbour's
property, fishing with my brother for the speckled browns,
my cast leapt back up the wet bank
& caught his eye.
How he cried out & I was afraid before I saw him,
wanting to change what I knew had happened,
wanting the cry to be a bird.
In some dreams the fish are tinsel in the trees,
the fish are cardboard painted brightly,
the fish smell bad when they fry
if they come from the sewer pipe, where they'd rest sometimes.
It softened their flesh,
when fresh caught
they were already rotten, you could put your hand
into their fishy sides.

We believed this.
In the dark, feeling our hands on the ice flow,
climbing the cliff away from the river,
our pants crusted with cold, hard,
the sound of the ice breaking in the darkness below.
Restless pain of which I am speaking.
In the mornings, I am drugged with salt & cold.
Some of the fish have scales that must be removed before eating
Some of the fish are rising with their teeth in black rows.
My hands grip into the softness of their gills.
My fingers are wet & the gills lift open, involuntary.
It is what the pain allows.
It is the start of food.

Toxicity

Can acupuncture cure the sadness of organs
Can the liver forget sadness when the needles enter,
its field of memory,
words of politic, the mining this week of the ports
of Nicaragua, Corinto & Puerto Sandino
Nicaragua of the liver & the pancreas,
Nicaragua of the heart,
the small cells of the kidneys teeming
The cords of energy severed in the body,
the body poisoned by underwater mines
In a country never seen, fish boats
pulling drag-nets under water,
risking explosion,
can acupuncture cure the sadness of the liver, now?

What is fucked-up in the body, what is blocked
& carried rolled in the intestine,
what suffocates so badly in the lungs,
adhering, we talk about it, *toxicity*, your body standing
at the sink & turned to me,
near but not near enough, not near enough, Gail
What if the blocked space in the liver is just sadness,
can it be cured then?
Can the brain stop being the brain?
Can the brain be, for a few minutes, some other organ,
any organ, or a gland, a simple gland with its fluids,
its dark edges light never enters, can it let us alone?
When I think of the brain I think
how can something this dark help us
together
to stay here, as close as possible, avoiding underwater minefields,
the ships of trade churning perilously toward us,
the throb of their motors calling the mines up,
as close as our two skins

Gale Force

In your mouth my sentence begins
to say *sentence*
as if there were no more quaver
in the air between our mouths
& our speeches were all invented
at the end of a railway platform in the weeds
Now part of our body, my breast touches
sentence under the skin,
between our mouths, folding
Force of sentence

In your mouth my sentence opens, kissing you with its noise,
where I am no longer sleeping
where the railway has ended & waves loosely
in the heat risen up between the weeds
I dream
two women in the strange yard washing the trees,
having washed each single tree
it is daylight;
the wrung-out rags spread on their shoulders
to dry
Our tough reusable wings

In your mouth my sentence is periodically sentence,
my skin crying short uttered joy:

it is out loud

it is out noise

it is over there & here

Heat risen past us, *gale force*, the trees
shining bright in the yard,
between our bodies,   pale wings,   & the railway

Blindness

Some of our desires are known only on the floor
of oceans, the nets dragged thru,
a light beyond colour we can't imagine, where we live now,
people of the surface,
whose foetuses still bear gills for a few days
& lose them, our kinship,
the water inside women,
water where we form & grow.

The halibut frozen whole, a sheet of memory,
held up, thawed, cut into slices
across the body, the central location of the spine,
our shared spine,
small bone hands of its vertebrae,
evolved away from us.

To feed us, first & lastly, taste
of white flakes upon the tongue,
soft resistance to the teeth & jaw;
our body is water &
the fish burn in it like fuel.

The flatfish that begins like any other,
swims upright
buoyant in the water, one eye on each side
of the head.
Then adolescent, feeling the body stagger
& list, gone sideways, one eye
migrates across the forehead or
thru the skull
to the right or left side, depending on the species.

Some of our desires are known only here,
are only now being let loose & admitted,
have only this moment stopped being
ashamed,
ashamed of the shape our bodies took & stayed on land
when the fish said No & went back
into the water,
mistake, mistake, fuck the lungs, some of our desires
are known only on the ocean floor, in the head

of the flatfish, halibut lying on its left side,
the eye that migrated across its skull
staring upward with the other.
At rest with it, patient.
Some of us have lungs that suffocate in the air.
The human body, two eyes fixed in the skull,
a third eye that presses on the forehead
& gets nowhere, presses & lives,
its silence the silence under oceans,
in the deep water of the body,
its blind side facing the brain

Eight Tests For Breathing

1

Stoop of the bronchial body
in the red brick building
Philosophy
To use well what is
if it is little

Say only meaning & go on
The heart can't read possibility
sick & tired
hurts me

2

Shut up if I do skip words
I can't breathe
I can't stop
breathing

3

Little & sick again
a dressing gown with red cats
Billy & Kenny
my brothers
their voices at distance, high giggles
I hang onto them, home from school, unseen
Another day past
I want them to argue
so I'll hear them longer
before they're gone
screen door slammed again

4

Bricks the building block of language
Grew up learning it
My mother gave me words
from the torn linoleum where she stood
before the sink
Later she worked outside
against my father's wishes
She bought linoleum & a new sink
I don't recognize
I can't believe I learned to read
there

5

Short lines
mince words
Struggle to get up & pee again
hot body waiting to catch breath
in the greying hall

6   *End The Arms Race Day, April 24 1982*

In the North I am where my life
solves with little pain
I think careful in my airless brain
communicate, try
Bloody Americas
who kill the witnesses, the mouths blown up
I can't breathe enough
to speak against human enemies
The armaments
If I'm sick
& don't say
Absolve me

7

In a far-off room
my family, eating dinner
The sound of their plates, mouths, evening
converse

My place empty

The windows of my bed
too high
The bricks darkening
Cool air outside, & family, & me
craving speech like all others

I want to grow up now
& breathe easy

Say it's worth it, kiddo

8

There is measure
the throat takes
& knows not
A measure like a step back
on a scaffold

These nights I risk to breathe
I dream
the workmen take down the scaffolding
around my building
red brick
Turning the braces, opening vise
upon vise
carefully wrenching the rods apart,
the boards that held them
stacked dirty
So few words
Little breath

The same old lungs' hurt & damage
& can't be cured
The breath there is
as the hands flutter
is poetry

Outside the poem, the scaffolds down at last
The building stands cleanly